VIETNAM 1939–75

FOUNDATION

CONTENTS

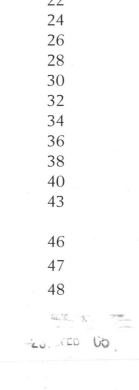

Key Issue

- Why were the French defeated?

When the Second World War broke out, the countries we now call Vietnam, Laos and Cambodia were called 'French **Indo-China**'. Although there was a Vietnamese 'Emperor' (called Bao Dai), the French had in fact conquered the area in the 19th century, and they were the real rulers.

INDO-CHINA OCCUPIED

French Indo-China was the world's third biggest grower of rice.   It also had coal and rubber.

Japan – which had few **natural resources** and a big population – wanted to conquer the area.   So, when Germany defeated France in 1940, the Japanese moved their army in and started taking what they wanted.   The French still ruled the area, but they could not stop the Japanese taking so much that, in 1945, around two million Vietnamese people starved to death.

THE VIETMINH

In 1941, Vietnamese **nationalists** started to fight for the **independence** of Vietnam.   They wanted a Vietnam free from both the French and the Japanese.   At first, they were based in south China.

The freedom fighters called themselves the **Vietminh**.   They were led by two Vietnamese **communists** – Ho Chi Minh and Nguyen Vo Giap (a history teacher).

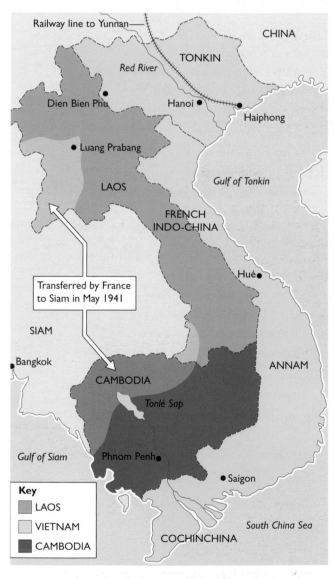

Indo-China was too far away from France for the French to defend it, so it was easily overrun by the Japanese army in 1940.

HO CHI MINH

Ho Chi Minh was born in 1890. His early life was amazing. He worked as a schoolteacher in Vietnam, then travelled the world as a seaman. From 1915–17 he worked as a pastry cook in a London hotel and then spent six years working as an odd-job man in Paris. In Paris he became leader of a group of Vietnamese people who wanted Vietnam to become independent.

In Paris, he also became a communist, and in 1929 he founded the Indo-Chinese Communist Party.

AMERICAN HELP

During the war, the Vietminh made **guerrilla** attacks on the French and Japanese in North Vietnam. They got help from the Americans, who trained them and gave them weapons. By 1945, the Vietminh had about 5000 soldiers, led by Giap.

THE DEFEAT OF JAPAN

By 1945, the Japanese were losing the war. They killed or imprisoned all the French officials in Indo-China, and tried to set up a pro-Japanese '**puppet state**', led by Bao Dai, the Emperor of Vietnam.

However, in August 1945 the Japanese were defeated.

Ho Chi Minh (centre) was a modest man who lived a simple life. He played down his communist beliefs, because he knew they would stop many people joining him. Above all else he wanted an independent Vietnam.

In 1945 in Vietnam there was a **power vacuum**. The Japanese had got rid of the French, and now the Americans had got rid of the Japanese. The Vietminh were the ONLY military force left! So Ho Chi Minh quickly took over Vietnam, including the two main cities of Hanoi (in the north) and Saigon (in the south). He said that Vietnam was a free, **democratic republic**. At first, Ho Chi Minh was supported by the Americans, who believed that the Vietnamese had the right to rule themselves.

THE FRENCH RETURN

The French, however, did not agree that Vietnam should become independent. They sent a force of 50,000 professional soldiers under General Jacques Leclerc to re-conquer the country.

The French fought a traditional war, attacking the Vietminh and driving them back. The Vietminh forces – led by Giap – fought a guerrilla war, waiting until the French army had moved on, then moving back into the area it had left. The French did not have enough troops to keep the areas they captured (the Americans had the same problem 20 years later). As one Vietminh fighter said of this time, 'We couldn't protect the villages, the French couldn't hold them.'

In March 1946 Ho Chi Minh went to Paris, and agreed a ceasefire with the French. For a while it looked as though he might be able to set up an independent Vietnam. But in November the French broke the ceasefire and drove the Vietminh back into the jungle.

> **Controversy!**
> 'France, Japan, America – NONE of them had any right to rule over Vietnam. If I was Vietnamese, I would have fought for independence too.'
> **What is your INSTANT REACTION?**

IMPACT OF THE COLD WAR

At the same time, the Americans changed sides. This was the time of the Cold War between America and communist Russia, and America was doing everything it could to stop the spread of communism. Ho Chi Minh was a communist, so America said he must be stopped. In 1950–53 America fought the Korean War to stop communist North Korea conquering South Korea; in the same period, America gave the French $3 billion to help them stop the Vietminh conquering Vietnam.

In 1949, however, the Chinese communists, led by Mao Zedong, took over China. This was a great help to the Vietminh because – just as America was helping the French – Mao supplied the Vietminh with guns and artillery.

'ELEPHANT FIGHTS GRASSHOPPER'

Ho Chi Minh always said that the Vietnamese fighting the French was like a grasshopper fighting an elephant. Because of Chinese help, however, this was not true. By 1950, the Vietminh army was 100,000 strong, and well-supplied with modern weapons. Against them, the French had an army of 100,000 French troops supported by 300,000 Vietnamese soldiers – but they were trying to control an area of thick forest the size of England. It was an impossible job.

When the Vietminh tried to attack the cities, they were defeated. But, hiding in the jungle, the Vietminh could make hit-and-run attacks on French patrols; when they did this the French could not stop them. By 1954, the Vietminh controlled all the countryside; the French only held the cities and some military **outposts**.

DIEN BIEN PHU

In January 1954, Giap began building up a huge army of 60,000 men and 200 artillery guns round the French outpost of Dien Bien Phu. Secretly, the Vietminh dug long tunnels to get close to the French lines.

In March 1954, Giap attacked. Anti-aircraft guns cut off the 13,000 French soldiers from help. There was desperate hand-to-hand fighting. By 7 May 1954 only 10,000 French troops were left alive, and half of them were wounded. The French surrendered and were sent to **concentration camps**.

A SOURCE

In 1986 the historian Robin Corbett wrote the following about Giap's preparations at Dien Bien Phu.

The Vietminh carried Chinese artillery guns piece by piece on their backs over what the French thought were uncrossable mountains. Giap used the artillery to destroy the French airfield – after that, the French could only send men and supplies by parachute. The loss of the airstrip meant that the French were bound to be defeated.

B SOURCE

In 1994 the historian Stanley Karnow wrote the following about Giap's preparations at Dien Bien Phu.

It was a terrible job for Giap's men to get their artillery and anti-aircraft guns into place in the hills round Dien Bien Phu. They dragged them there by sheer muscle-power. By the middle of January, the Vietminh had 50,000 men; the French had 13,000.

C SOURCE

In 1982 the historian Richard Natkiel wrote the following about Giap's preparations at Dien Bien Phu.

When the Vietminh attacked in March 1954, the French had about 18,000 soldiers. But Giap had many more men, and good artillery and anti-aircraft guns. First, he destroyed the airstrip: supplies had to be parachuted in, which was very dangerous.

D SOURCE

Vietminh soldiers taking supplies to Dien Bien Phu by bicycle.

E SOURCE

This map shows the areas of Vietnam controlled by the Vietminh in 1949.

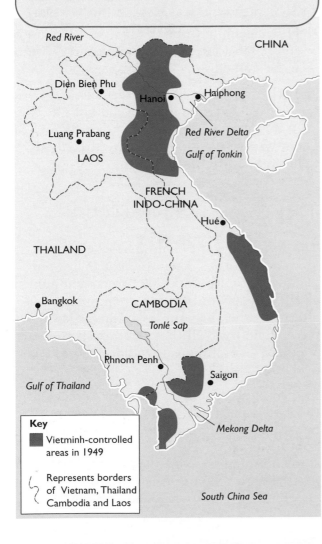

Key

▓ Vietminh-controlled areas in 1949

⌇ Represents borders of Vietnam, Thailand Cambodia and Laos

F SOURCE

In 1994 the historian John Grenville wrote the following about the war between the French and the Vietminh.

The French found that they could not defeat the Vietminh. By 1952 they had lost 90,000 dead, and the French people were beginning to complain. The French generals were not as good as Giap.

Questions

a What can you learn from Source A about the position of the French defenders at Dien Bien Phu?

b Does Source C support the evidence of Sources A and B about the battle for Dien Bien Phu?

c How useful are Sources D and E as evidence of the strengths of the Vietminh forces?

d 'The French were defeated at Dien Bien Phu because they under-estimated the Vietminh.' Use the sources and your own knowledge to explain whether you agree with this view.

Key Words

Geneva Agreement • 17th parallel • Diem • domino theory • re-education • Buddhists • land issue • elections • murders • National Liberation Front • Kennedy • 'Vietcong' • 'military experts'

THE GENEVA AGREEMENT

On 8 May 1954 (the day after the surrender of Dien Bien Phu) a Conference was held at Geneva to make peace for **Indo-China**. Five countries were present – America, Britain, France, Russia and China – as well as the **Vietminh**, and people from Cambodia, Laos and French-held Vietnam.

After difficult talks, on 21 July 1954, a Final Agreement was produced. It said:

- Vietnam would be split along the 17th **parallel**.
- Vietminh forces would pull out of South Vietnam, and French forces would pull out of North Vietnam.
- North Vietnam would be controlled by Ho Chi Minh. South Vietnam would be ruled by Ngo Dinh Diem (a Vietnamese nobleman who had worked for Bao Dai).
- **Free elections** would be held in Vietnam by July 1956 to decide how the country would be re-unified.

Nobody signed the Final Agreement. America openly rejected it, and Diem did not intend to keep it. Most of all, neither America nor Diem wanted elections, because they thought that Ho Chi Minh would win.

THE DOMINO THEORY

The Americans at this time believed in the 'domino theory'. They thought that if one country in South East Asia turned **communist**, all the others would fall to communism, one after the other, like a row of dominoes. They were afraid that – if the communists took over Vietnam – communism would go on to take over the world.

Instead of accepting the Geneva Agreement, the Americans made it clear that they wanted to set up a strong anti-communist state in South Vietnam. They were determined to stop communism in Vietnam at the 17th parallel. So they promised to prop up Diem's government with money and weapons.

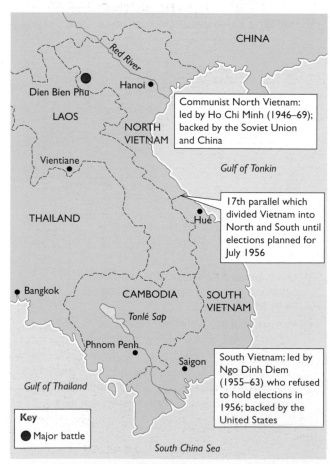

CHINA

Red River

Dien Bien Phu

Hanoi

LAOS

NORTH VIETNAM

Communist North Vietnam: led by Ho Chi Minh (1946–69); backed by the Soviet Union and China

Vientiane

Gulf of Tonkin

17th parallel which divided Vietnam into North and South until elections planned for July 1956

THAILAND

Hué

Bangkok

CAMBODIA

SOUTH VIETNAM

Tonlé Sap

Phnom Penh

Saigon

Gulf of Thailand

South Vietnam: led by Ngo Dinh Diem (1955–63) who refused to hold elections in 1956; backed by the United States

Key
● Major battle

South China Sea

Vietnam after the Geneva Agreement, July 1954.

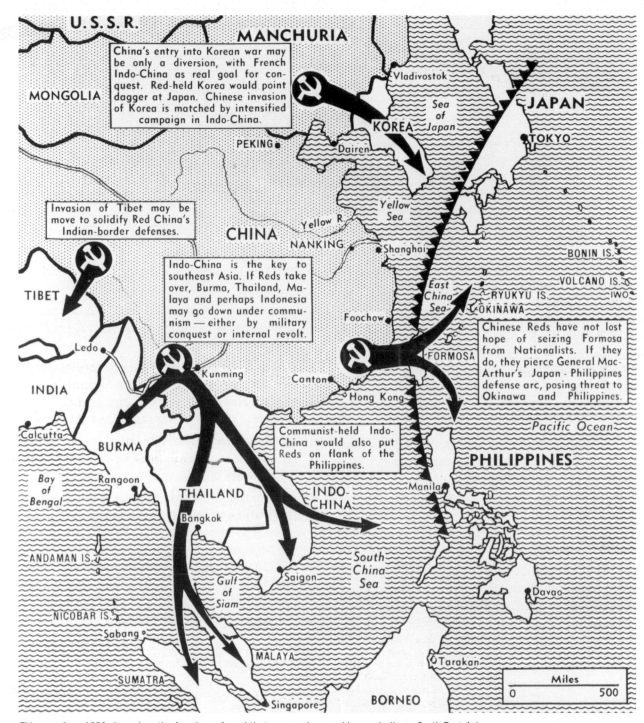

The map contains the following labels and text boxes:

U.S.S.R.

MANCHURIA

MONGOLIA

China's entry into Korean war may be only a diversion, with French Indo-China as real goal for conquest. Red-held Korea would point dagger at Japan. Chinese invasion of Korea is matched by intensified campaign in Indo-China.

Vladivostok

JAPAN

Sea of Japan

KOREA

TOKYO

PEKING

Dairen

Yellow Sea

Invasion of Tibet may be move to solidify Red China's Indian-border defenses.

CHINA

NANKING

Yellow R.

Shanghai

BONIN IS.

VOLCANO IS.

IWO

TIBET

Indo-China is the key to southeast Asia. If Reds take over, Burma, Thailand, Malaya and perhaps Indonesia may go down under communism — either by military conquest or internal revolt.

East China Sea

RYUKYU IS.

OKINAWA

Foochow

Chinese Reds have not lost hope of seizing Formosa from Nationalists. If they do, they pierce General MacArthur's Japan - Philippines defense arc, posing threat to Okinawa and Philippines.

Ledo

Kunming

Canton

FORMOSA

INDIA

Calcutta

Hong Kong

Communist-held Indo-China would also put Reds on flank of the Philippines.

Pacific Ocean

BURMA

PHILIPPINES

Bay of Bengal

Rangoon

THAILAND

INDO-CHINA

Manila

Bangkok

ANDAMAN IS.

Gulf of Siam

Saigon

South China Sea

Davao

NICOBAR IS.

Sabang

MALAYA

Tarakan

SUMATRA

Singapore

BORNEO

Miles

0   500

This map from 1950 shows how the Americans feared that communism would spread all over South East Asia.

'DEMOCRACY' DIEM-STYLE

In October 1955, Diem held elections in South Vietnam only. He did very well – in the capital city of Saigon (where there were 450,000 voters) 605,000 people voted for him! He claimed to have 98 per cent of the votes (the Americans made him reduce it to a more believable 70 per cent). Clearly Diem had cheated in the elections.

Controversy!

'It was not only the Americans who ignored the 1954 Geneva Agreement. The Chinese and Russians ignored it too. The Vietminh had no intention of stopping fighting. The spread of communism was a fact, not a theory, and the Americans were right to be worried.'

What is your INSTANT REACTION?

The Americans said they would win over the 'hearts and minds' of the South Vietnamese by showing them how good the American way of life was.

'RE-EDUCATION'

Diem was a cruel and unpopular ruler:

- Most Vietnamese were Buddhists; Diem was a Catholic, who killed and imprisoned hundreds of Buddhists.

- Land issue: during the war, a lot of land had been freed up because the owners had fled or been killed. In North Vietnam, Ho Chi Minh gave this land to the peasants. In South Vietnam, Diem gave it to his rich Catholic landowner friends. They made the peasants pay high taxes and work for them for free.

- Diem hunted down South Vietnamese people who supported the Vietminh and 're-educated' them in prison camps. 12,000 Vietminh who would not change their views were executed.

The Americans did not like what Diem was doing, but they had to support him, or the communists would take over. So Diem did as he liked – as one American put it, Diem was: 'a puppet who pulled his own strings – and ours as well.'

Controversy!
'Diem was a bad ruler.
The Americans were morally wrong to support him, however bad they thought communism was. They were on to a loser from the start.'
What is your INSTANT REACTION?

THE WAR BEGINS AGAIN

The date for all-Vietnam elections came and went. In the south, Diem was killing the Vietminh and oppressing the peasants. So:

- In 1959, Ho Chi Minh ordered the Vietminh in South Vietnam to start killing government officials (in the next two years, 8000 were murdered).

- In 1960, Ho Chi Minh set up the **National Liberation Front** (NLF). It did not just include communists – it was a **patriotic** movement to get rid of Diem, and to re-unite north and south Vietnam. Many middle-class people (such as doctors and teachers) supported it, as well as the peasants and communists.

America was determined to stop the North Vietnamese. In 1960 John F Kennedy became President of America, and he had promised to get tough on communism. He did not, however, want to push things so far that he started a world war with Russia or China, so the Americans:

- Started calling the Vietminh the '**Vietcong**' (it made them sound more communist, and less patriotic).

- Sent 'military experts' to train and 'advise' the South Vietnamese army. By 1963, there were 16,000 of these 'experts' – the first American soldiers in Vietnam.

A SOURCE

In 1994 the historian Stanley Karnow wrote the following.

One of Kennedy's advisers said that one day there would be 300,000 American soldiers in Vietnam. Kennedy laughed and said: 'You're crazy – that will never happen'.

B SOURCE

In 2002 the historian Andrew Wiest wrote this.

December 1967: there were 500,000 American soldiers in Vietnam.

Make notes on the following and explain how they affected the situation in Vietnam:
   'The domino theory'
   'Re-education'
   'Military experts'.

Questions

a How did the domino theory help to bring about America's involvement in Vietnam?

b Sources A and B give different views about the extent of American involvement in Vietnam. Why do you think they are different? Explain your answer using Sources A and B and your own knowledge.

c How useful is Source C to an historian studying the effects of the war on the people of South Vietnam? Use Source C and your own knowledge to answer this question.

d Why did the United States become involved in the conflict in Vietnam? You may refer in your answer to:
   • The defeat of the French
   • The domino theory
   • Diem's policies in South Vietnam
   Explain your answer.

C SOURCE

South Vietnamese from the village of An Hoa waiting to be rescued after their village was destroyed (November 1967).

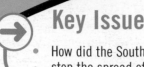

Key Issue

- How did the South Vietnamese try to stop the spread of communism?

Key Words

ARVN • strategic hamlet programme • corrupt officials • Vann • 'get on team' • 'hearts and minds'

In 1961, the Americans spent $270 million propping up the Diem government. They were paying, among other things, for the South Vietnamese army (the **ARVN**). There were 170,000 ARVN soldiers, compared to perhaps just 10,000 **Vietcong** – but the ARVN still could not defeat them.

The problem was the peasants – they were helping the Vietcong, giving them food and information. The Americans asked Diem to try to solve this problem.

THE 'STRATEGIC HAMLET' PROGRAMME

Diem borrowed an idea which the British had used to defeat the **communists** in Malaya – in 1962 he introduced the 'strategic hamlet' programme.

The idea was to move people away from areas where the Vietcong were strong, and to re-house them in villages protected by moats and fences (so that the Vietcong could not get in). Then the villagers would be given things like farm aid and medical care – paid for by America – so that they would come to like the South Vietnam government and stop supporting the communists. By 1963, two-thirds of the South Vietnamese had been moved into these 'strategic hamlets'.

The programme was a disaster. The peasants hated having to move home to a place far away, and then build new homes and set up defensive ditches and fences.

Also, the South Vietnamese were angered because government officials stole the money given by the Americans, and made them pay

for the new houses and aid that they were supposed to be getting for free.

The strategic hamlet programme made MORE people support the Vietcong, not less.

'GET ON TEAM!'

At the same time, the ARVN was losing the war. Colonel John Paul Vann was the chief American adviser in Vietnam; in 1963 he gave up his job, saying that the ARVN soldiers were no good and that their commanders were cowards. The Americans covered this up, so as not to upset Diem.

The American government did not want people back home to know what was going on. The Americans were bombing Vietcong areas, and flying ARVN soldiers into combat zones, but the government pretended that their soldiers were just 'advisers'. Most of all, the government did not want people to know that the war was going badly – newspaper reporters who asked questions about losses were told simply to 'get on team' (be loyal).

A SOURCE

In 1994 the historian Stanley Karnow wrote the following.

The strategic hamlet programme turned the peasants into Vietcong supporters. They resented having to work without pay to dig moats, plant bamboo stakes and put up fences against an enemy who was not attacking them. Also, they were angry at corrupt officials who stole money meant for seed, medical care and education.

B SOURCE

In 1990 the journalist Neil Sheehan wrote the following.

The peasants were enraged. Their houses were torn down or burned, and they had to pay to build new houses which were not as good as the old ones. Local officials sold them metal roofing given free by the Americans. They were angry at the long days of forced work, digging a moat round the village, and putting up barbed-wire fences and bamboo stakes.

C SOURCE

In 1986 the historian Robin Corbett wrote the following about the strategic hamlet programme:

The idea was to move people to safe homes, defended by barbed-wire fences and ditches filled with sharpened sticks. They would be given medicine and education to win their 'hearts and minds'. It was a disaster. The strategic hamlets were like concentration camps.

D SOURCE

A South Vietnamese bus driver describes a Vietcong assassination.

Five or six Vietcong guys stopped my bus and looked at everybody's identity cards. They dragged two men off the bus, saying: 'We warned you to give up your job, but you haven't listened; so now we're going to carry out the sentence'. They cut off the men's heads and pinned a note to their shirts, saying that they were policemen working for the South Vietnam government.

Then the Vietcong guys gave everybody back their identity cards, saying: 'You will get into trouble with the government if you do not have these'.

E SOURCE

A Vietnamese woman is held captive by an American soldier.

F SOURCE

A South Vietnamese soldier questions a man suspected of being Vietcong.

Questions

a What can you learn from Source A about the strategic hamlet programme?

b Does Source C support the evidence of Sources A and B about the strategic hamlet programme?

c How useful are Sources D and E as evidence about why the Vietcong were able to win the support of the South Vietnamese people?

d 'The South Vietnamese peasants supported the Vietcong because they were ill-treated by the government of South Vietnam.' Use the sources and your own knowledge to explain whether you agree with this view.

Key Issue

- Why was Diem overthrown?

Key Words

Quan Duc • flags • Catholics • Buddhists • Van Minh • Ngo Dinh Nhu • coup d'état (1963) • Johnson • Nguyen Khanh (1964)

DEATH BY BURNING

The date is 11 June 1963. A 66-year-old Buddhist monk named Quan Duc sits down in the middle of a busy Saigon crossroads. He crosses his legs and puts his hands together to pray. Another monk pours petrol over him. Quan Duc strikes a match and sets fire to himself. For ten minutes he sits still as the flames cover him; then his body topples over . . .

You may wonder whether it was worth dying in such a terrible way – but Quan Duc's death changed the history of Vietnam. An American photographer, tipped off before the event, was there to take the photograph which shocked the world. It was the first time that many Americans realised how unpopular Diem's government was.

BUDDHIST OPPOSITION

South Vietnamese law said that people could only fly one flag – the flag of Vietnam. But, as we have seen, Diem was a Catholic; so when Catholics flew the flag of the Catholic Church, nothing was done.

In May 1963, however, when some Buddhists flew the Buddhist flag to celebrate Buddha's birthday, troops fired at them, killing nine people, eight of them children. When 10,000 Buddhists went on a protest march about this, thousands of their leaders were arrested – leading to Quan Duc's horrific protest in Saigon.

The American government protested, but Diem just ignored them. He said the Buddhists were **communists** trying to cause trouble, and his sister-in-law, Madame Nhu, told American officials: 'If the Buddhists want another barbecue, I will be glad to give them the petrol and a match.'

THE COUP D'ÉTAT

The Americans realised it was time to stop supporting Diem. On 2 September 1963, President Kennedy publicly attacked Diem on TV, saying that he had 'gotten out of touch with the people', and calling for 'changes in policy and people'. He knew that some generals in the **ARVN**, led by Duong Van Minh, were plotting to take over the government. The **CIA** had been helping them, on Kennedy's orders.

In Saigon, Diem's ruthless brother and chief adviser, Ngo Dinh Nhu, tried stop the plot, but unfortunately he told his plan to one of the plotters. On 1 November 1963, therefore, the rebel generals moved quickly and took over the government.

THE DEATH OF DIEM

At first, the generals planned merely to force Diem and Nhu to leave the country, but they managed to escape. Diem phoned the Americans to ask for help, but was told that nothing could be done. Next day, he and his brother surrendered. They were picked up by an army car, tied up and shot.

President Kennedy had not wanted this, and was upset by the news. Three weeks later, Kennedy, too, was assassinated, and Lyndon B Johnson became President in his place.

THE BULLY AT THE PORCH

Led by General Minh, the new government tried to get the South Vietnamese people back on its side. It set free the Buddhists who were in prison. It said that it wanted the **Vietcong** to live peacefully in South Vietnam, and that it would ask the American troops to leave.

This was not what the Americans wanted to hear. President Johnson believed in the domino theory: 'If you let a bully come into your garden, next day he'll be in your porch, and the day after that he'll rape your wife.'

The Americans wanted the South Vietnamese government to do more to stop the spread of communism. So it supported a second plot, which brought General Nguyen Khanh to power in 1964.

But the new government found it could do little to win the war. The Vietcong were growing more powerful all the time. In 1957 there had only been 2000 Vietcong in South Vietnam and even by January 1963 there were still only 23,000.

But Diem's anti-Buddhist policies had led more people to join the Vietcong, and by January 1965 there were 170,000 Vietcong soldiers fighting in South Vietnam.

B SOURCE

President Eisenhower wrote this letter to Diem in October 1954.

I want to help you to set up a strong government, with an army which will be able to stop the spread of communism. I hope that this help, together with your efforts, will keep Vietnam free. Such a government, I hope, would be loved by its people, so that the communists would not dare to try to force their beliefs on your free people.

C SOURCE

October 1963: a Buddhist monk burns himself to death as a protest against Diem's government.

A SOURCE

A Buddhist monk remembers the following about Diem's government.

Diem's anti-Buddhist policies made me angry. In 1955, the government forbade us to celebrate Buddha's birthday . . . I organised a big march, but – two miles down the road – the police were waiting for us. They just surrounded the first 100 marchers and arrested us.

Questions

a Why was the United States so concerned about Diem's government?

b Sources A and B give different views on the government of Diem. Why do you think they are different? Explain your answer using Sources A and B and your own knowledge.

c How useful is Source C to an historian studying the opposition to Diem among the people of South Vietnam? Use Source C and your own knowledge to answer this question.

d Why did the United States government turn against President Diem? You may refer in your answer to:
  • America's concerns about the spread of communism
  • Diem's unpopularity
  • The need for a more effective anti-communist policy in South Vietnam.

Key Issue

→

- Why did America send combat troops to Vietnam?

Key Words

radar • USS *Maddox* • flying fish • attack on airbases (Feb 1965) • Operation Rolling Thunder

Until 1964, although America had sent many 'advisers' to Vietnam, the Americans were still not directly fighting the North Vietnamese. That changed in August 1964, when the 'Gulf of Tonkin incident' brought America into the war.

The incident started on 31 July 1964 when South Vietnamese **commandos** attacked North Vietnamese radar stations. They were helped by the American warship, the USS *Maddox*. Because of this, on 2 August 1964, three North Vietnamese torpedo boats attacked the *Maddox*. They failed to do any damage – two torpedoes missed, the other failed to explode, and American planes sank one torpedo boat and damaged the other two. President Johnson ignored the attack, as there were no American losses.

DUMB SAILORS AND FLYING FISH

On the night of 3 August 1964, however, the captain of the *Maddox* reported that he was being attacked again. No sailor heard enemy gunfire or saw an enemy boat. American pilots flying overhead did not see any enemy boats. But for four hours the *Maddox* fired wildly into the darkness.

President Johnson knew that there had not been an attack – he said: 'those dumb, stupid sailors were just shooting at flying fish'. But there was an election due in November, and Johnson had to act tough on **communism**. The pilots changed their reports, and said there had been an attack. Johnson ordered American planes to bomb North Vietnamese navy bases.

On 7 August 1964, Johnson told Congress that an attack had taken place – and they gave him

power to do 'anything necessary' to defend freedom in South East Asia.

VIETCONG ATTACKS

At first, Johnson did not attack North Vietnam. But then:

- In December 1964, the **Vietcong** completely destroyed the best two units of the South Vietnamese army (proving that the **ARVN** could never defeat the Vietcong on their own).

- In February 1965, the Vietcong attacked American air bases, destroying ten helicopters, killing eight Americans and wounding more than 100.

An American adviser shows ARVN soldiers how to use a bayonet. Bayonets were useless in Vietnam – the soldiers used them for opening cans of fruit.

FLIES AND THE MANURE PILE

Johnson said: 'We are swatting flies when we should be going after the manure pile'.

- On 13 February 1965 he ordered 'Operation Rolling Thunder' (bombing North Vietnamese targets).
- In March 1965, American soldiers were sent to Vietnam to protect American air bases. By the end of the year, there were 200,000 American soldiers in Vietnam.

America had entered the war.

A SOURCE

An article, written in 1994 by two journalists, for a website which fights for true reporting in the press.

On August 4, the American government claimed that North Vietnamese torpedo boats had attacked American ships in the Gulf of Tonkin. President Johnson ordered American bombers to retaliate

It was a lie. It never happened. James Stockdale, a Navy pilot who watched it all said: 'they were firing at ghosts – there was nothing there but water'. In 1965, President Johnson said: 'For all I know, the navy was shooting at whales out there'.

B SOURCE

President Johnson's speech to Congress, 5 August 1964.

Last night I told the American people that the North Vietnamese had attacked American ships, and that I had therefore ordered our planes to attack North Vietnamese gunboats and ports. This has been done, and a lot of damage has been done to their boats and bases. Two American planes were shot down.

C SOURCE

Wrecked planes on an American air base in Vietnam after a Vietcong attack in February 1965.

Questions

a Why did Johnson change his policy over the two Gulf of Tonkin incidents?

b Sources A and B give different views on the Gulf of Tonkin incident. Why do you think they are different? Explain your answer using Sources A and B and your own knowledge.

c How useful is Source C to an historian studying the reasons Johnson sent troops to South Vietnam in 1965? Use Source C and your own knowledge to answer this question.

d How important was the Gulf of Tonkin incident as a reason for the US sending combat troops to South Vietnam? You may refer in your answer to:
- How the incident led to US troops being sent to South Vietnam
- The impact of the domino theory
- Johnson and his political opponents in the US.

Key Issue
- What tactics did each side use?

Key Words

NVA • Vietcong guerrillas • Westmoreland • 'search and destroy' • 'kill ratio' • booby traps • 'Bouncing Betty' • hit-and-run • Zippo raids • frustrated • unpopular jobs • small arms fire • cluster bombs • napalm • Ia Drang (1965)

'Operation Rolling Thunder' was supposed to last eight weeks. In the end, it went on for more than three years.

It was a failure. The Americans hoped that it would destroy North Vietnamese **supply lines**, and that the sheer size of the bombing would frighten their opponents into surrender. They were wrong. The North Vietnamese had few factories or military bases to bomb; so most of the bombs fell into fields and forests and had no effect at all.

SEARCH AND DESTROY

On the ground, the North Vietnamese posed two threats:

- the regular **North Vietnamese Army** (NVA) in the north
- the **Vietcong guerrillas** in the south.

The American commander General Westmoreland left the South Vietnamese **ARVN** to tackle the Vietcong guerrillas. To fight the NVA, he decided on a policy of 'search and destroy' – American troops were sent out on missions to find and kill enemy army units.

This policy, too, was a failure. Most times, American troops did not even see the enemy, yet they were the victims of booby traps and hit-and-run raids.

Frightened and frustrated, they destroyed villages instead – American soldiers called their raids 'Zippo raids', after the name of the cigarette lighters they used to set fire to Vietnamese houses.

UNPOPULAR JOBS

The three most unpopular jobs were:

- radio operator
- machine gunner
- walking point (leading the platoon, checking for enemies and booby traps).

Both the radio and machine gun weighed three times more than a rifle, and these soldiers were always the ones the enemy killed first in an ambush.

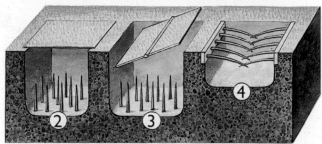

Vietcong booby traps:
(1) bamboo stakes on a trip wire;
(2) and (3) pits;
(4) a leg-trap (the curved spikes made it difficult to pull the leg out).

SMALL ARMS

More than half the American soldiers who died in Vietnam were killed by small arms fire (pistols, rifles and machine guns). There were few big battles. Most of the fighting was raids and ambushes, involving only a few dozen men on each side.

BOOBY TRAPS

Eleven per cent of American deaths were caused by booby traps. The North Vietnamese soldiers:

- Put sharpened bamboo stakes in pits for American soldiers to fall into (see page 16). Sometimes they put manure on the stakes, so the wounds would become infected.
- Set trip wires (especially in water) which would explode a grenade.

MINES

The North Vietnamese soldiers also planted mines. The most frightening of these was 'Bouncing Betty', which, when you trod on it, jumped up about a metre and exploded at the top of your legs.

The mines and booby traps did not win the war, but they frightened and frustrated the American soldiers, who were fighting an enemy they could not see.

Controversy!

'The Americans were criticised for the way they waged the war, but the Vietcong were as bad – in different ways. The Americans used **napalm** and Agent Orange; the Vietcong had booby traps and "Bouncing Betty" mines. They were both as bad as each other.
Both sides used morally indefensible weapons. Vietnam merely proved that you cannot have a "civilised" war.'
What is your INSTANT REACTION?

A wounded American soldier being taken to army hospital in 1968. Both Americans and Vietcong tried to recover the bodies of their dead. The Americans thought it was good for morale. The Vietcong wanted to hide the number of their men who were being killed from the Americans.

WAR FROM THE AIR

The Americans fought back using bombing raids:

1. Cluster bombs (called 'mother bombs' by the Vietnamese) exploded in the air, breaking into 600 smaller bombs. When these hit the ground, they exploded into thousands of pellets. They were designed not to kill but to maim and injure – and to flood North Vietnamese hospitals with wounded. Later, the Americans made the pellets from plastic, so they wouldn't show up on an X-ray; doctors had to spend hours digging around in the victims' flesh to find the pellets.
2. Napalm bombs showered burning petroleum jelly over the victims. It stuck to the skin and burned at 800°C.

To protect themselves, the North Vietnamese dug hundreds of miles of tunnels, and hid in these. In the end, bombing failed to win the war for the Americans.

THE FIRST BATTLE

At the beginning of the war, in November 1965, the Americans trapped the NVA in the Ia Drang Valley in South Vietnam. They fired 33,000 artillery shells and 7000 rockets. The NVA fled into Cambodia, having lost 1800 men dead, compared to only 240 Americans.

But in the end, Ia Drang was a disaster for the Americans. It made General Westmoreland think that the policy of 'search and destroy' was the right one. The 'kill ratio' – one American for every eight **communists** – was very high, and he believed that such huge losses would force the North Vietnamese to give up.

He was wrong. The North Vietnamese were so determined to win that they did not mind the losses.

Instead, 'search and destroy' cost too many *American* lives, and in the end it was the American public that wanted to give up.

THE NVA

Also, the battle of Ia Drang taught the NVA that they could not beat the Americans in a head-on battle. So they changed their tactics. Instead, they ambushed the American search and destroy raids. They developed the tactic of 'clinging to the belt' (close-range fighting), so that the Americans did not dare to use **artillery** and planes for fear of hitting their own men.

A SOURCE

Trinh Duc, who had been a Vietcong soldier, remembers how they fought the Americans (1996).

There was no way we could stand up to the Americans – when they attacked we just ran away from them. But when they turned round, we followed them . . . The Americans' way of fighting was to attack, then call for back-up from their planes and artillery. We would disappear if we could, but if we couldn't we moved very close to them, so the planes could not get at us.

B SOURCE

In 2002 the historian Andrew Wiest wrote this.

The Vietcong had a policy of 'hanging on to American belts'. They got as close as possible to the American soldiers before opening fire. If they were close enough, the Americans could not use their artillery and planes for fear of hitting their own men.

C SOURCE

In 1990 the journalist Neil Sheehan wrote the following about the battle of Ia Drang in 1965.

The cruel struggle started. Vietnamese and Americans killed each other within yards. This meant that the Americans could not use their planes and artillery, and the Vietnamese stayed as close to the Americans as possible, a tactic they called 'clinging to the belt'.

D SOURCE

An American soldier carries a Vietnamese woman out of a combat zone.

E SOURCE

An American soldier wrote the following to his parents about the treatment of Vietnamese civilians (1967).

We kill civilians by accident and on purpose – and that's just plain murder. We make more Vietcong than we kill by the way we treat these people. Some of the things that happen here would make you ashamed of good old America.

F SOURCE

American troops on a 'search and destroy' mission – a soldier uses his Zippo lighter to set fire to a Vietnamese peasant's home.

Questions

a What can you learn from Source A about communist combat tactics against the Americans?

b Does Source C support the evidence of Sources A and B about communist combat tactics against the Americans?

c How useful are Sources D and E as evidence of US treatment of Vietnamese civilians?

d 'The tactics used by the communist forces were more appropriate than those of the Americans for the Vietnam War.' Use the sources and your own knowledge to explain whether you agree with this view.

Make notes on:
- Search and destroy
- The Vietnamese way of fighting
- The American way of fighting
- The Battle of Ia Drang and its results.

Key Issue

- How did the Americans view their enemy?

Key Words

'sneaky' • 'animals' • 'snakes' • 'slant-eyed' • body count • torture • Agent Orange • massacres and atrocities • Varnado Simpson

Most American soldiers respected the **North Vietnamese Army** (NVA); they wore uniforms and fought bravely in a 'fair fight'.

Many American soldiers, however, hated the **Vietcong**, who wore the black civilian 'pyjamas' of Vietnamese peasants, and fought using 'sneaky' **guerrilla** tactics.

BODY COUNT

The American commander, General Westmoreland, was obsessed by the enemy 'body count' (how many soldiers were killed). He believed that, if the enemy suffered big losses, they would eventually have to give up the war. To do this, he sent out American patrols as bait, hoping that they would be attacked by the NVA or Vietcong. The attacked patrol then had orders to call in air strikes or **artillery** fire.

The Americans never knew how many enemy they killed, however, because the North Vietnamese took their dead away with them. So the Americans often just made up the numbers of enemy dead.

Wounded prisoners were usually shot by both sides. Healthy prisoners were taken back for questioning – and torture.

DEFOLIANTS

Frustrated that the enemy was hiding in the jungle, the Americans started using defoliants (chemicals to kill off the plants). The most-used defoliant was Agent Orange which, it was discovered later, led to deformed births and caused cancer in soldiers on both sides.

After a while, the Americans started using Agent Orange on the villagers' crops in Vietcong-controlled areas. It forced the villagers to move away to new areas, and the Americans thought it would separate them from the guerrillas. In fact – because most Vietcong were villagers – all it did was move the Vietcong into new areas.

A SOURCE

An American soldier remembers what he thought about the Vietnamese people.

We were taught that they were animals. We were told that kids and women were your enemy. We never trusted any of them. I hated anything with slanted eyes before I went over there. You always thought they were snakes – sneaky, which they are. Slant-eyed people, you couldn't trust them.

B SOURCE

An American soldier in South Vietnam wrote the following to his parents in 1968.

I am filled with respect and hate. Respect because the Vietcong are good fighters – they know they cannot stand up to us in a fire fight. But hatred for the Vietnamese, because they come round selling us Coke and beer, and then they run back to the Vietcong and tell them how many we are, where we are, and where our leaders are.

SOURCE

An American soldier remembers what he thought about the enemy soldiers.

I respected the NVA. They put on a uniform and came at you head-on. There was honour between us and them. But the Vietcong didn't stand up and fight like men. It was real easy for me to think of the Vietcong as animals.

D **SOURCE**

A Vietcong guerrilla, terribly wounded in the stomach, had carried his intestines around in a bowl for three days. When a South Vietnamese soldier refused him a drink, an angry American soldier gave him his canteen, saying: 'Any soldier who can fight three days with his insides out can drink from my canteen anytime.'

E **SOURCE**

Varnado Simpson, one of the members of Charlie Company at My Lai, admitted the following in 1989.

That day in My Lai, I killed about 25 people. Me. Men, women. Shooting them, cutting their throats, scalping them, cutting off their hands and cutting out their tongue. I did it . . . My mind just went.

And I wasn't the only one that did it. Once I started, the training, the whole unthinking part of killing, it just came out.

F **SOURCE**

A photograph of a dead NVA soldier.

Questions

a What can you learn from Source A about how US troops were trained to see the Vietnamese?

b Does Source C support Sources A and B about US attitudes towards the enemy?

c How useful are Sources D and E as evidence of the attitudes of US troops towards the enemy?

d 'The American soldiers hated the enemy.' Use the sources, and your own knowledge to explain whether you agree with this view.

8 THE SOLDIERS' WAR

Key Words

drafted • blacks, Hispanics and poor whites • 58,000 dead • one-year tour of duty • 'cherries' • inexperienced • fragging • drugs • draft-dodging • desertion • DEROS

STATISTICS

Around 2.8 million Americans served in Vietnam. At first, many were volunteers. After 1966, however, most were '**drafted**' (conscripted). Their average age was 19.

Many white and rich Americans managed to avoid the draft – young men at university could delay call-up until they had finished their degree. For this reason, most **infantry soldiers** in Vietnam were blacks, Hispanics (Spanish Americans) and poor whites. The men served a 'tour of duty', which lasted just one year.

In total, 58,000 Americans died in Vietnam – about two per cent of those who went. Overall, American soldiers had a one in fifty chance of dying, and a one in ten chance of being wounded. But only about 10 per cent of the soldiers ever saw combat, so the chances of a combat soldier being killed were 20 per cent (one in five), which is high.

Of those killed in combat in Vietnam, 43 per cent were killed in the first three months of their tour, when they were inexperienced. Only six per cent died in the last three months (when they were being careful and trying to get home safely).

TRAINING: 'KILL A GOOK EVERY DAY'

American soldiers called the enemy 'gooks', 'dinks' and 'slopes' (from the shape of Vietnamese people's eyes). They were trained to think of the enemy as animals – it made it easier to kill them.

'CHERRIES'

General Westmoreland thought that a one-year tour of duty would keep the men's spirits up. He was wrong. The one-year tour of duty system greatly harmed the American army in Vietnam – by the time a soldier had learned how to survive and fight, he went home.

Platoons were always getting new, inexperienced men. They were called 'cherries', and they were distrusted. Many were new men for friends who had been killed. Worse than that, they made mistakes which cost lives – often their own, but possibly yours. At the same time, soldiers at the end of their 'tour' wanted to avoid combat and risks; they were not reliable either.

'FRAGGING'

Many soldiers came to hate their officers, who sometimes tried to get on in the army by scoring high body counts in combat; the soldiers thought they were helping their career by endangering soldiers' lives. Sometimes, the men killed their officer (this was called 'fragging'). During 1970–1 about 700 officers were killed by their own men, and overall about three per cent of all officers who died in Vietnam were killed by their own troops.

DRUGS

Many soldiers took drugs – cannabis, cocaine and heroin were used during R&R ('rest and recreation'). 'Speed' was used to stay awake during night-time raids, or just to 'get high'.

In 1971 in Vietnam, 5000 soldiers were treated in army hospital for combat wounds, and 20,000 for drug abuse.

WHAT WAS US MORALE LIKE?

Having read this chapter, you will probably already have come to a conclusion about American morale. **Draft-dodging**, fragging and drugs are all evidence of low morale. So is **desertion**; in the period 1966–73 there were 503,926 incidents of desertion and draft-dodging, although some of these were repeat offences.

At the start of the war, morale was good, because many men were volunteers who believed in what they were fighting for.

By the end of the war, however, most soldiers were draftees, who hated the war, knew people back home did not support them, and were just counting the days to DEROS (Date Eligible for Return from OverSeas).

C SOURCE

Communist soldiers bring supplies to the South from North Vietnam.

A SOURCE

An officer in the **North Vietnamese Army** remembers how he felt about the war.

We hated the enemy so much, and were so keen to free our people, that we felt we could overcome any difficulty and make any sacrifice. We were defending our country and punishing the enemy.

Our propaganda helped us to believe in the cause we were fighting for.

B SOURCE

President Johnson said the following to Congress in August 1964.

The free nations of South East Asia are in danger. North Vietnam wants to take over South Vietnam and Laos.

As President of America, I have decided to ask Congress to help me make it clear that all such attacks will be opposed, and that America will help the free nations of the area to defend their freedom.

Questions

a What were the weaknesses in America's conscription policy?

b Sources A and B give different views about the war in Vietnam. Why do you think they are different? Explain your answer using Sources A and B and your own knowledge.

c How useful is Source C to an historian studying how the Vietcong were kept supplied during the war? Use Source C and your own knowledge to answer this question.

d How good was the morale of US troops in Vietnam? You may refer in your answer to:
 • Conscription
 • 'Fragging'
 • Drug abuse
 • Motivation.

On 31 January 1968 – the Vietnamese New Year (or Tet holiday) – the **Vietcong** made a huge attack on 100 towns and cities in South Vietnam.

At first the Vietcong were very successful. The Americans were completely taken by surprise, and half the **ARVN** were on holiday. However, it was a war neither side were used to fighting. The Vietcong changed their usual hit-and-run tactics and fought to the death. In the end, they were defeated.

AIMS OF THE TET OFFENSIVE

The **communist** government in North Vietnam had two aims:

• They hoped that the people of South Vietnam would rise up and overthrow their government, and that the ARVN would give up and surrender.

• They hoped that the Americans would realise that they could not win the war, and would give up and go home.

In the end, the government and army of South Vietnam did not collapse. And the Americans did not go home. However, the Tet Offensive did give the Americans a shock. During the Offensive, a 15-man Vietcong suicide squad captured the American embassy in Saigon, and held out for six hours. Many Americans saw this on TV, and public opinion began to turn against the war – Americans began to realise that they could not win the war.

Some historians say that, although the Vietcong were defeated, the Tet Offensive was the turning point in the war.

HORROR IN HUÉ

In the north of South Vietnam, the Vietcong captured the city of Hué. It took the ARVN and American soldiers 25 days to recapture the city. In the meantime, however, the Vietcong had executed about 3000 civilians who had links with the South Vietnamese government.

This massacre was used by the American government to persuade the public that the war had to go on.

MILITARY CONSEQUENCES

The Tet Offensive was a defeat for the North Vietnamese, and a disaster for the Vietcong. The Americans lost just 1500 dead, and the ARVN just 3000 – one tenth of the losses suffered by the communists.

Most of the 45,000 North Vietnamese killed were Vietcong, including many of their best **guerrilla** fighters, and most of their leaders. This meant that new leaders from North Vietnam had to be sent to run the Vietcong. It took the North Vietnamese four years to recover from the Tet Offensive.

A SOURCE

In 2002 the historian Andrew Wiest wrote the following about the Tet Offensive.

The Tet Offensive was a total failure and a demoralising defeat for the communists. Nearly 58,000 of the 84,000 troops were killed, and the Vietcong were almost wiped out. The communists had hoped that the ARVN would surrender, but they had fought well. Yet, surprisingly, it was the start of the communists' victory.

B SOURCE

In 2002 the historian Vivienne Sanders wrote the following about the Tet Offensive.

The North Vietnamese had hoped that the South Vietnam government would collapse, and the Americans would go home. Instead, the communists suffered big losses. The Tet Offensive was one of those rare battles where both sides lost.

C SOURCE

In 1986 the historian Robin Corbett wrote the following about the Tet Offensive.

Overall, the North Vietnamese came out best from the Tet Offensive. The South Vietnam government did not collapse, as some had hoped. But those who thought that the Offensive would weaken the Americans' will to fight were happy with the results of Tet.

D SOURCE

American soldiers hide from enemy fire during the Tet Offensive.

E SOURCE

Huong Van Ba, an NVA artillery officer in the Tet Offensive, said the following to an American interviewer.

After the Tet campaign, we didn't have enough men left to fight a battle, only enough to make hit-and-run attacks. Morale was low because so many men had been killed. We spent a lot of time hiding in tunnels. Many soldiers deserted, and young people in the North did not want to join the army.

F SOURCE

A map showing the Vietcong attacks during the Tet Offensive.

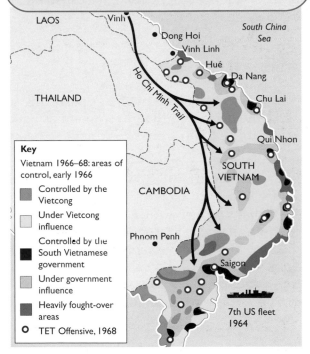

Key

Vietnam 1966–68: areas of control, early 1966

- Controlled by the Vietcong
- Under Vietcong influence
- Controlled by the South Vietnamese government
- Under government influence
- Heavily fought-over areas
- ○ TET Offensive, 1968

7th US fleet 1964

Questions

a What can you learn from Source A about the Tet Offensive?

b Does Source C support the evidence of Sources A and B about the Tet Offensive?

c How useful are Sources D and E as evidence about the Tet Offensive?

d 'The Tet Offensive was a disaster for the communists.' Use the sources and your own knowledge to explain whether you agree with this view.

Key Issue

- Did the media affect the war's outcome?

Key Words

Life • Credibility gap • Harrison Salisbury • Tet • Saigon Embassy • Walter Cronkite • Saigon Police Chief • Johnson (1968)

To begin with, American newspapers and television supported the war. In 1965 *Life* magazine said: 'This war is worth winning'. Two years later, however, *Life* magazine wrote that North Vietnam was not a danger to America, and that the war was not worth the deaths of young Americans. The media had turned against the war.

THE CREDIBILITY GAP

It was not just that the media opposed the war. Worse, they exposed the government as liars, who kept the truth from the American people.

For instance, the American government had always claimed that they were bombing military targets in North Vietnam, and that few civilians were harmed. In 1966, the North Vietnamese let the journalist Harrison Salisbury, from the *New York Times*, go to Hanoi. He reported on the damage that was being done to civilians by American bombs (some of which were falling on hospitals and schools).

The American government and army commanders such as General Westmoreland believed that the media were turning the public against the war. In August 1967, for the first time, an opinion poll showed that more people were against the war (46 per cent) than were for it (44 per cent).

THE IMPACT OF TET

Vietnam was the first war that had a lot of TV coverage, and this had a big effect on people.

The Tet Offensive was particularly powerful:

- Many Americans, watching the **Vietcong** suicide squad capture the American Embassy in Saigon, felt like Walter Cronkite, the TV reporter: 'What the hell is going on? I thought we were winning this war'.

- As a cameraman was filming a Vietcong prisoner, the Saigon Police Chief walked over and shot him in the head (see Source C). The man was later proved to be a member of a Vietcong murder squad; but all the viewers saw was a man horribly executed without trial. Many Americans decided that the South Vietnamese government was not worth saving.

- President Johnson lost popularity, and decided not to stand in the Presidential election of 1968.

During the Tet Offensive, a 15-man Vietcong suicide squad took over the American embassy in Saigon. They were killed, but the attack shocked and demoralised the American public.

A SOURCE

In 1979, General Westmoreland said the following about the role of the American media in the war.

The news media supported the opponents of the war in America, and backed up the message that the war was 'immoral'.

In the Tet Offensive of 1968, the Vietcong suffered such a defeat that it took them four years to recover.

But the reports of the Offensive by the newspapers and television gave the impression of an endless war that could never be won.

B SOURCE

In 1994, the historian Stanley Karnow wrote the following about the role of the media in the war.

Opinion polls at the time showed that the Tet Offensive did not change American attitudes to the war. Public support for the war had been falling steadily for two years before Tet, because of the increasing deaths, rising taxes, and the feeling that the war would go on for ever.

During Tet, Americans rallied behind their government. Afterwards, they began to despair as the fighting dragged on.

Questions

a To what extent did the communists achieve their aims for the Tet Offensive?

b Sources A and B give different views of the role of the US media during the Tet Offensive. Why do you think they are different? Use Sources A and B and your own knowledge to answer this question.

c How useful is Source C to an historian studying the Tet Offensive? Use Source C and your own knowledge to answer this question.

d 'The United States were clearly losing the war by early 1968.' Do you agree? You may refer in your answer to:
- Why the US entered the war
- How successful US tactics were
- The impact of the Tet Offensive.

Make notes on the following and explain how they damaged the morale of the American people:
- The credibility gap
- The writings of Harrison Salisbury
- The Saigon Embassy raid
- The execution by the Saigon Police Chief.

C SOURCE

The Saigon Chief of Police kills a Vietcong prisoner during the Tet Offensive.

11 MY LAI

Key Issue

- How did My Lai affect the United States?

Key Words

Charlie Company • Lieutenant William Calley • 347 • rapes • Hugh Thompson • cover-up • Ron Haeberle • Seymour Hersh • 'rotten and anti-American'

On 16 March 1968, during the Tet Offensive, an American patrol led by Lieutenant William Calley entered the Vietnamese village of My Lai. The village was in a **Vietcong**-held area, and the American base nearby was under attack.

The patrol did not find any Vietcong, and did not come under enemy fire. Instead, it committed the worst reported American atrocity of the war, murdering 347 men, women, children and babies. Some of the women were raped first, then killed. One soldier admitted killing babies clinging to their mother because, he said, the babies were about to attack.

Only an American helicopter pilot, Hugh Thompson, who saw the massacre, tried to stop the killing and save the villagers.

IMPACT OF MY LAI

At first there was a cover-up. The government kept the massacre a secret – the official report said that the patrol had killed 90 Vietcong, with one American casualty – a soldier shot in the foot. (This soldier later admitted shooting himself to try to excuse the murders.)

Even when news got out about the massacre, little was done. Only Calley was convicted – of the murder of 22 villagers – and sentenced in 1971 to life imprisonment.

GOOD GUYS AND BAD GUYS

Most Americans did not want to think about the massacre. Seymour Hersh, the journalist who first heard the story, had trouble finding a newspaper to publish it. Many people said that the newspaper which eventually published pictures of the massacre (taken by the official army photographer) was 'rotten and anti-American'.

In one poll, half the people refused to believe that a massacre had happened at all. Some defended Calley because he was fighting for his country. Others said the massacre just showed how inhuman war was. Fewer than one in 14 people agreed with Calley's sentence. After less than four years, President Nixon pardoned him and set him free.

Americans were used to seeing films with actors like John Wayne, who played good and honest heroes. They thought of themselves as 'the good guys', and wanted to believe that the Vietcong were 'the bad guys'. It had been bad enough to find out that their South Vietnamese allies could shoot a prisoner in cold blood. That their own American soldiers might also be committing atrocities was unthinkable.

A SOURCE

This report about My Lai was printed in November 1969 in the American magazine *Time*.

The short action at My Lai, a village in Vietcong-infested territory 355 miles north-east of Saigon, may affect the war. According to reports on TV and in the newspapers, a company of 60 or 70 American soldiers went into My Lai early one morning, and destroyed its houses, animals and everybody they could find for 20 minutes. At least 100 men, women and children were killed, perhaps many more.

B SOURCE

In 2002, the historian Vivienne Sanders wrote the following about the My Lai massacre.

The most famous, but not the only, example of American hatred of the Vietnamese was the massacre of My Lai on March 16 1968. 347 unarmed civilians were killed: old men, women, teenagers and even babies. Women were raped and shot. Animals were dropped into the wells to poison the water.

C SOURCE

This account of the My Lai massacre is from the website of an American radio and TV station.

On March 16 1968 the angry and frustrated men of Charlie Company went into the village of My Lai, in a Vietcong area. The 'search and destroy' mission turned into the massacre of over 300 unarmed civilians including women, children, and old people. According to eyewitnesses, old men were bayoneted, praying women and children were shot in the head, and at least one girl was raped and then killed.

D SOURCE

A photograph taken at My Lai by Ron Haeberle, the official army photographer.

E SOURCE

A My Lai villager who survived remembered the following about the massacre.

Nguyen Khoa, a 37-year-old peasant, told of a 13-year-old girl who was raped before being killed.

The American soldiers then tore off his wife's clothes and began to rape her – but their six-year-old son, riddled with bullets, fell and covered her with blood, so the soldiers left her alone.

F SOURCE

Hugh Thompson was given the Soldier's Medal in 1998 for 'heroism above and beyond the call of duty' for his actions at My Lai in 1968.

Questions

a What can you learn from Source A about the events at My Lai?

b Does Source C support the evidence of Sources A and B about the events at My Lai?

c How useful are Sources D and E as evidence about the events at My Lai?

d 'The events at My Lai showed the US army to be bloodthirsty killers.' Use the sources and your own knowledge to explain whether you agree with this view.

12 THE WAR AND CIVIL RIGHTS

Key Issue

- How did the Civil Rights Movement affect the war?

Key Words

Civil Rights Movement • segregation • drafted • twice as likely to be killed • Martin Luther King • Nation of Islam • Muhammad Ali (1967) • in the field • behind the lines

BLACK INEQUALITY

Slavery was abolished in America in 1863, but black people did not get equal rights with the whites. Especially in the American South, black people were not allowed to use the schools, restaurants, toilets or even drinking fountains that white people used; this was called **segregation** (keeping apart).

After the Second World War, things began to change. In 1948, President Truman abolished segregation in the army, saying that black and white soldiers had to fight side by side. And in the 1960s the **Civil Rights Movement** grew up – led by a pastor called Martin Luther King – to get equal rights for black people.

Because fewer young black people went to university, it was harder for them to avoid the **draft** (see Chapter 8). So a young black man was almost twice as likely to have to go to Vietnam as a young white man. Also, in Vietnam, at first, black soldiers were twice as likely to be killed as white soldiers. The government managed to get this figure down, but not before black Civil Rights leaders accused them of sending black soldiers to the most dangerous areas.

NATION OF ISLAM

Many black people began to say that the war was wrong. A Muslim group called the 'Nation of Islam' opposed the war. Why, they asked, should American blacks fight for a country which did not give them equal rights? Why should they go to the other side of the world to kill another group of coloured people? 'No **Vietcong** ever called me a nigger,' said one Civil Rights leader.

The world champion boxer, Muhammad Ali, was a member of the Nation of Islam. In 1967 he was drafted, but refused to go to fight in Vietnam. He was stripped of his world title and banned from boxing.

MARTIN LUTHER KING

In 1967, Martin Luther King also said that he thought the Vietnam War was wrong. After that, most black people in America were much more interested in gaining civil rights than in winning the Vietnam War.

RACE IN THE FIELD

In the early years of the war, black and white soldiers were all professionals, and they worked well together. Later on, when most soldiers were draftees, the problems got worse. On the front line ('in the field') soldiers worked together because they had to – their lives depended on it. But, behind the lines, there was a lot of racial conflict.

A SOURCE

A black soldier remembers what it was like between black and white soldiers in Vietnam.

One guy in our unit was a keen member of the Ku Klux Klan. That hacked a lot of us off, because the black and white soldiers in our unit worked really well together. There was racism behind the lines, but not in the fighting units, because we had to rely on each other in the field.

B SOURCE

A white soldier remembers what it was like between black and white soldiers in Vietnam.

There was always a chance of trouble between blacks and whites.   As soon as there was an argument between a young white man and a black man, the name-calling started and then fists started flying.

I saw this happen in the field, as a matter of fact.

C SOURCE

A white soldier remembers what it was like between black and white soldiers in Vietnam.

There was always trouble just under the surface.   In the field, people needed each other, so they got along pretty well.

But, behind the lines, there was trouble. Blacks and whites who were friends in the field could not be friends behind the lines.

D SOURCE

An anti-war protest meeting in 1971.

E SOURCE

A speech by Martin Luther King in 1967.

The government sends more young black men to die in Vietnam than the rest of the population.

It is a cruel joke that we have to watch young black and white boys on TV – killing and dying together for a country which will not let them sit together in the same school.

F SOURCE

A black soldier helps a wounded white soldier in the field in 1968.

Questions

a What can you learn from Source A about relations between black and white soldiers in Vietnam?

b Does Source C support the evidence of Sources A and B about relations between black and white soldiers in Vietnam?   Explain your answer.

c How useful are Sources D and E as evidence of attitudes to the war in the United States?

d 'Racism was a major problem among US troops in Vietnam.'   Use the sources and your own knowledge to explain whether you agree with this view.

Key Issue

• In what ways did people oppose the war?

Key Words

burning draft cards • Martin Luther King • Great Society • Johnson • $20 billion • Tet Offensive • protests • Cambodia (1970) • Kent State University • Operation Phoenix

By the late 1960s, many Americans were against the war:

• Some were on the Vietnamese side, saying that they ought to be able to do as they want in their own country.

• Some thought that the war was a waste of money, which should be spent on America's poor people.

• Some were Christians who said that all war was wrong.

• Many people said that Vietnam was not worth the deaths of young Americans.

BURNING DRAFT CARDS

When the government wanted a young man to fight in Vietnam, it sent him a **draft** card. Many young men ignored it. Some burned their cards in public. When the government tried to arrest them, they ran away to countries such as Canada.

MARTIN LUTHER KING

After 1967, the **Civil Rights** leader Martin Luther King spoke out against the war. He told young black men to refuse to go into the army.

In 1964, President Johnson had promised Americans a 'Great Society' programme to help the poor. He had promised poor people welfare payments and good homes. But the Vietnam War was costing Johnson $20 billion a year, and, to pay for it, he was forced to stop the Great Society programme. Martin Luther King believed that this money should have been spent helping America's poor.

JOHNSON QUITS

In March 1968, President Johnson told Americans that he was not going to try to stay on as President. People were angry with him for stopping the Great Society programme and the Tet Offensive had made him look as though he was losing the war. Johnson knew he would lose the 1968 election.

This was a huge success for the anti-war protesters. There were many anti-war marches in 1969 and 1970, and in 1971 half a million people took part in a march in Washington, led by hundreds of Vietnam veterans (men who had fought in Vietnam). When there was a pro-war demonstration a fortnight later, only 15,000 turned up. However, Richard Nixon, who became President in 1968, still continued the war.

Anti-war protesters call President Johnson a 'war criminal' in October 1967. Protests like this made Johnson realise that he would not be re-elected as president in 1968.

KENT STATE

In 1970 Nixon ordered American troops to invade Cambodia, to kill **Vietcong** fighters hiding there.

Thousands of students went on protest marches. In one of these, at Kent State University in Ohio, four students were shot dead.

'OPERATION PHOENIX'

In 1968, the American government set up 'Operation Phoenix'. In the next three years the **CIA** killed more than 20,000 Vietcong suspects in South Vietnam, and arrested and imprisoned 28,000 more. The operation had some success – 17,000 Vietcong changed sides and started to support the South – but the US was accused of setting up 'death squads'.

A SOURCE

A speech by Martin Luther King in 1968.

We are protecting a bad government that harms poor people. It costs half a million dollars to kill a Vietcong soldier, but we are only spending $53 on every poor American back home.

How arrogant we are – fighting for the so-called freedom of the Vietnamese 10,000 miles away, when there is so much to do in our own country!

B SOURCE

President Johnson explains why he ended the Great Society programme.

I knew that I would lose power at home if I stopped the Great Society programme to fight that bitch of a war on the other side of the world. But if I let the communists take over in South Vietnam, I would have looked a coward, America would have looked weak, and we would not have been able to do anything anywhere in the world.

C SOURCE

This American newspaper cartoon from 1972 shows President Nixon as a bad angel.

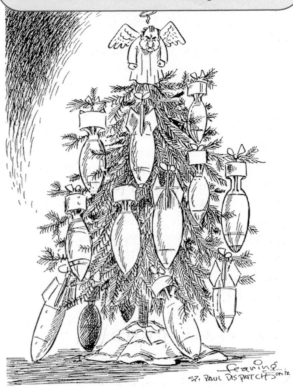

Questions

a Why did President Johnson decide not to stand for re-election in 1968?

b Sources A and B give different views of the Vietnam War. Why do you think they are different? Use Sources A and B and your own knowledge to answer this question.

c How useful is Source C to an historian studying American attitudes to the war? Use Source C and your own knowledge to answer this question.

d Why did opposition to the war increase? You may refer in your answer to:
   • News of the My Lai massacre
   • Student protests
   • Cost of the war.

14 VIETNAMISATION

In May 1968 peace talks started in Paris to try to end the Vietnam War. The American government wanted to get out of the war, but President Nixon promised that he would only accept 'peace with honour'. So the talks got nowhere.

There were two main sticking points:

- The North insisted that Vietnam had to be re-united; America would only accept a peace which kept South Vietnam as a separate country.
- The North insisted that the **National Liberation Front** should be part of the government of South Vietnam; America would only accept peace if North Vietnamese troops left South Vietnam.

VIETNAMISATION

President Nixon and his adviser Henry Kissinger said they wanted to 'de-Americanise' (or '**Vietnamise**') the war – they meant that they wanted to leave the fighting to the South Vietnamese. Nguyen Van Thieu (the leader of the South Vietnam government after 1967) did not trust them – he thought the Americans were getting ready to abandon him.

Nixon hoped he could get 'peace with honour' by doing three things:

- Continuing the peace talks.
- Gradually withdrawing American troops from Vietnam, while supporting the South Vietnam government with weapons and aid.
- Bombing North Vietnam.

Nixon's policy did not work. The North Vietnamese government knew that the anti-war movement in America was growing stronger, and that Nixon was desperate to get out of Vietnam. All they had to do was to wait – one day the Americans would *have* to pull out, and then they could defeat the **ARVN** easily.

PEACE AGREEMENT

In October 1972, in Paris, Kissinger worked out a peace agreement with the North Vietnamese. It said:

- The fighting would stop.
- Each side would keep the land it held.
- American troops would leave Vietnam.
- The North Vietnamese would set free 700 American prisoners of war.
- Elections would be held in South Vietnam to choose a new government.

Thieu, the South Vietnamese leader, was angry. He thought the Americans were abandoning him. He refused to sign the agreement. So the North Vietnamese also left the talks.

In December 1972 Nixon acted. American planes bombed North Vietnam for 11 days. They dropped more bombs than in the three years 1969–71. The North agreed to re-open the talks.

Then Nixon told Thieu that he was going to sign the peace agreement whether the South Vietnam government agreed or not. Thieu gave in, and the Paris Peace Agreement was signed on 27 January 1973.

A SOURCE

In 2002 the historian Andrew Wiest wrote the following about the situation in 1973.

*In 1973, it looked as though the South Vietnamese could win. They had one million soldiers with the latest American weapons, against 150,000 **Vietcong**.*

The South Vietnam government was weak and corrupt, but in 1973 America sent $2,300,000 in aid to South Vietnam.

B SOURCE

In 2000 the historian Ray Bowers wrote this.

*In 1973, the **NVA** had not been driven out of South Vietnam. About 145,000 **communist** troops controlled a third of the land and 5% of the people. American troops and aid were the South Vietnam government's only hope of surviving.*

C SOURCE

In 1994 the historian Stanley Karnow wrote this.

The communists were determined to take over South Vietnam. Led by Thieu, the government was weak, corrupt and unable to stop them. Nevertheless, it had American weapons and American aid, and it controlled 75% of South Vietnam's land and 85% of its people. Against it were only 150,000 North Vietnamese.

Questions

a What can you learn from Source A about the situation in South Vietnam when the peace agreement was signed?

b Does Source C support the evidence of Sources A and B about the situation in South Vietnam when the peace agreement was signed?

c How useful are Sources D and E as evidence of the success of Nixon's policy in Vietnam?

d 'Nixon's policy in Vietnam was a success.' Use the sources and your own knowledge to explain whether you agree with this view.

D SOURCE

An American cartoon from 1972.

E SOURCE

An American pilot is set free from a North Vietnamese prison camp in 1973.

F SOURCE

In 1983 an American history book said the following about the peace.

Nixon said it was 'peace with honour'. But the peace agreement shows he had been totally defeated. And the term 'honour' was inappropriate for a war which cost billions of dollars and the lives of 57,000 Americans and a million Vietnamese.

Key Issue

- Why did America lose?

Key Words

Diem • Thieu • land issue • strategic hamlets • My Lai • guerrillas • Russian anti-aircraft guns • morale • opposition in America

HEARTS AND MINDS

The Americans knew that they would only win the war if they won 'the hearts and minds' of the peasants of South Vietnam.

But the leaders of South Vietnam – like Diem and Thieu – would not take the land from their rich landowner friends and give it to the peasants. So they never gained the support of the peasants. And the Americans would not force the South Vietnam government to make land reforms. Instead they tried to move the peasants away from the **Vietcong** (the strategic hamlet programme – see Chapter 3) and ended up simply destroying peasant villages. This policy, and massacres like My Lai (see Chapter 11), made the peasants hate them.

So the peasants helped the Vietcong because they hated the Americans and the South Vietnam government – and America lost the war.

TACTICS

Another reason that the North Vietnamese beat the Americans was tactics. They knew they could never defeat the Americans in a head-on battle. So they used **guerrilla** tactics, and wore down the Americans' will to win.

Also, China and Russia supplied the North Vietnamese with weapons. Russian anti-aircraft guns were especially useful, because the Americans relied on helicopters and bombing raids.

MORALE

Another reason the North Vietnamese won the war was because the morale of their soldiers was so much better. The North Vietnamese were determined to drive the Americans out of their country. On the other side, many American soldiers were inexperienced **draftees** who did not want to be there, and 'fragging' and drug-taking are signs that their morale was poor. They had better weapons, but the enemy had more willpower.

OPPOSITION IN AMERICA

The most important reason America lost the war, however, was nothing to with the fighting in Vietnam. The Americans lost the will to continue, and President Nixon knew that he would never win the 1972 election unless he pulled out of the war.

A SOURCE

In 1986 the historian Robin Corbett wrote the following about why America lost the war.

The South Vietnam government was hopelessly corrupt and weak. Only American support kept it in power. The North Vietnamese Army had superb morale, discipline and leadership.

B SOURCE

In 2002 the historian Vivienne Sanders wrote the following about why America lost the war.

The communists were never going to give up. The Americans were fighting someone else's war, and their tactics made the Vietnamese hate them. The South Vietnam government was corrupt, weak and hated. After 1968 the morale of the American army fell.

C SOURCE

In 2000 the historian Gerard DeGroot wrote the following about why America lost the war.

The Americans did not use the wrong tactics, they helped the wrong side. The South Vietnam government was corrupt and cruel.

Also, the Americans faced a very strong enemy. The Vietcong were not a bunch of barefoot peasants – they were a determined and well-armed force which fought well in small battles.

D SOURCE

Anti-war protesters in Washington in 1969.

E SOURCE

In 1981 a Vietnam veteran suggested the following about why America lost the war.

The North Vietnamese out-psyched us. We had the military power, but we lost the war because we had not got the will-power. We defeated the Tet Offensive in 1968 but when they saw the opposition in America, and how they had toppled the President, they realised that they could make the Americans defeat themselves.

F SOURCE

Children run from their village after it had been bombed with **napalm** by American planes in 1972.

Questions

a What can you learn from Source A about why the United States lost the war?

b Does Source C support the evidence of Sources A and B about why the United States lost the war?

c How useful are Sources D and E as evidence about why the United States lost the war?

d 'The Americans lost the war in Vietnam because they lacked the will to win.' Use the sources and your own knowledge to explain whether you agree with this view.

Key Issue

• What happened after the Americans left?

Key Words

American withdrawal • Ho Chi Minh City • executions and re-education • communists • land • boat people • Agent Orange • unexploded bombs • Russian aid • Pol Pot (1978) • China invades (1979)

THE COLLAPSE OF SOUTH VIETNAM

After the Peace Agreement of 1973, fighting began almost immediately between North and South Vietnam.

The **ARVN** lost. On 30 April 1975, the Americans helicoptered out the last 6000 Americans in Vietnam. The **North Vietnamese Army** captured Saigon, and renamed it Ho Chi Minh City. Thieu escaped, and went to live in Britain.

The war had started in 1941, and had involved fighting the Japanese, the French and the Americans.

At last it was over.

POST-WAR VIETNAM

The North Vietnamese took revenge on their enemies. About 60,000 supporters of Thieu's government were put to death. Another 300,000 were sent away to **concentration camps** to be 'ic-educated'. The **communists** took the rich people's land and animals.

Many South Vietnamese tried to get out. In the next 15 years about 1.5 million 'boat people' set out to sea on rafts or in small boats, hoping to escape. Some drowned or were killed by pirates. Some were sent back, or ended up living in terrible refugee camps.

But about a million South Vietnamese people went to live in America or France.

US CHEMICAL WARFARE

The war left Vietnam with many problems, and – for more than 20 years after the war – Vietnam was one of the world's poorest countries:

• Huge areas of land had been ruined by Agent Orange (and still cannot grow crops).
• There were 17 million unexploded shells, mines and bombs left all over Vietnam – more than 2000 people have been killed or wounded trying to clear them away.
• The war had ruined Vietnam's economy, and the new government's communist policies did not help it to get going again.

Things got worse when Russia stopped sending economic aid in 1991. However, this forced the government to allow private businesses, and – in the last few years – things have got a little better for the Vietnamese.

FURTHER CONFLICT

North Vietnam's war with America and South Vietnam had ended in 1975, but the new government kept on fighting. In 1978, it invaded Cambodia to destroy the terrible government of Pol Pot.

This angered Cambodia's ally China, and in 1979 the Chinese invaded Vietnam. There was a short war, and the Chinese were driven back with heavy losses.

In 1989, the Vietnamese pulled out of Cambodia.

A SOURCE

The following is taken from an interview that Nguyen Van Thieu (South Vietnam's former ruler) gave to the American magazine *Time* in 1990.

Question: *South Vietnam was not a democracy when you were in power, was it?*

Thieu: *That is not true. Vietnam had been a democracy for hundreds of years. When I was in power we had democratic elections not only for the national government, but also at local and even village level.*

B SOURCE

In 2002, the historian Vivienne Sanders wrote the following about Thieu's government.

The South Vietnamese government had promised to hold an election in 1971. Thieu held an election, but he only allowed one candidate – himself!

Some people said that America should stop sending aid to South Vietnam, but President Nixon said that democracy took time to grow.

Questions

a How justified were the fears of some South Vietnamese that the communists would take bloody revenge against their enemies after they took over in 1975?
b Sources A and B give different views of Thieu's rule. Why do you think they are different? Use Sources A and B and your own knowledge to answer this question.
c How useful is Source C to an historian studying economic conditions in Vietnam in 1990? Use Source C and your own knowledge to answer this question.
d Why has the war continued to affect the people of Vietnam? You may refer in your answer to:
   • 'The boat people'
   • Effects of chemical warfare and munitions
   • Economic problems.

Controversy!

'Vietnam got its independence, but life got worse. The South Vietnamese were better off under the Americans.'
   What is your INSTANT REACTION?

C SOURCE

This picture shows South Vietnamese traders returning from China in 1991.

Key Issue

- How has the Vietnam war affected America?

Key Words

social problems • civil rights •
War Powers Act • Vietnam Syndrome •
veterans • baby killers • suicides •
Three Servicemen Memorial (1984)

The Vietnam War had a huge and disastrous effect on America:

- President Johnson's 'Great Society' programme had to be stopped to pay for the war. Many bad social and **Civil Rights** problems – poverty, slums, lack of medical care – were left to get worse.

- The war undermined the position of the President. It ruined Johnson's chances of re-election in 1968. And in 1973 Congress passed the War Powers Act, which took away the power of the President to go to war; it said he had to ask Congress before he could send American soldiers abroad.

The 1982 memorial to America's Vietnam War dead. All 58,000 names are recorded on these granite walls.

- The war bitterly divided Americans. Even in the 2004 election, candidates George Bush (who had not gone to Vietnam) and John Kerry (a Vietnam veteran) argued over the part they had played in the Vietnam War.

THE VIETNAM SYNDROME

Vietnam also had a huge effect on American foreign policy. For many years after the Vietnam War, Americans refused to take part in anything which did not affect America directly (this was called 'the Nixon doctrine'). For instance, America did nothing when Russia invaded Afghanistan in 1979. The Americans were worried that they might get drawn into another long, disastrous war. This feeling only came to an end in 1991, when America went to war against Iraq.

VETERANS

Three million Americans fought in the Vietnam War (the 'veterans'). Of these, half a million have suffered depression, drug addiction or divorce – and more have committed suicide than were killed in the war itself.

The veterans' biggest problem was that – when they returned from the war – they were not treated as heroes, but as 'baby killers'. They felt abandoned. Not until 1982 was a memorial built (see page 40) – three black stone blocks carved with the names of all the 58,000 Americans killed in Vietnam. This was not felt to be heroic enough, and in 1984 another memorial of Three Servicemen (see page 42) was added.

THE END

In 1985 an American veteran, William Ehrhart, went back to Vietnam, where he met a North Vietnamese general. Ehrhart asked: 'Could we have won if we had done things differently?'

The general said: 'Probably not. History was on our side. We were fighting for our country. What were you fighting for?'

Ehrhart answered: 'Nothing that really mattered'.

A SOURCE

David Donovan, a Vietnam veteran, wrote the following in 1985.

We were right to fight terror and what was being done to the poor and backward people of Vietnam. I do not agree with our accusers. We fought because it was our duty and our only cause was freedom. It was not an 'immoral' war at all – it was a good war gone terribly wrong. I loved the South Vietnamese people.

B SOURCE

A black American Vietnam veteran said the following about the war in 1984.

We were fighting for a lie. We were not there to protect democracy. We were not protecting America.

We were the last people to believe in the idea of 'a just war'. There is no honour in war.

C SOURCE

Another black American Vietnam veteran said the following about the war in 1984.

I promised myself in 'Nam that I was not going to die to protect anybody else's property. I will not fight to stop the spread of communism.

I'll fight anyone who attacks America. But if they come to try to send me to some other country, I'm going to have my gun ready for them.

E SOURCE

David Donovan, a Vietnam veteran, wrote the following in 1985 about the opening of the Washington memorial.

The place was crammed with people who reached out to shake my hand and slap my back. They were cheering and waving flags and shouting: 'Welcome home!'

I cried, but this time it was not from sadness – it was with happiness.

Questions

a What can you learn from Source A about this veteran's attitude to the war in Vietnam?
b Does Source C support the evidence of Sources A and B about the attitudes of veterans to the war?
c How useful are Sources D and E as evidence about the attitude of the American people to the war?
d 'American veterans think the war was a worthwhile cause.' Use the sources and your own knowledge to explain whether you agree with this view.

F SOURCE

A black American Vietnam veteran said the following about the war in 1984.

I was in Vietnam from 1968 to 1969. It was one hell of a time, good and bad, but I would not change it for anything. I gave my youth to fight America's enemies in a small country halfway round the world. We lost that battle, but we won the Cold War.

Controversy!
'The Vietnam War was unjust, and a wicked waste of lives and money. The presidents who supported it should be put in prison.'
What is your INSTANT REACTION?

How to write about sources is as important in the exam as knowing what happened. You must practise this until you can do it.

EDEXCEL

The sources on which these examples are based are on pages 28–29.

(a) What can you learn from Source A about the events at My Lai? (4)

TECHNIQUE

- To get more than two marks for this question you must make an inference (i.e. 'read between the lines' to write something that the source *suggests* or *implies*).
- Two inferences with some explanation will get full marks.
- Start each idea with the same phrase each time, for example, 'Source A suggests . . .'

Example: *Source A implies that the Americans massacred innocent people, because it says 'everybody they could find'. It also suggests that, because this story was on TV and in the newspapers, that the incident would reduce support for the war.*

(b) Does Source C support the evidence of Sources A and B about the events at My Lai? (6)

TECHNIQUE

- To get high marks, you must talk about *how much* the sources agree. It is a good idea to do this in a final sentence.
- Do not compare Source A with B. You will get no marks for this.
- Do not write about whether the sources are reliable or who wrote them. You will get no marks for this.
- Compare Source C with Source A, then compare Source C with Source B. Do not compare C with A and B together.

Example: *Source C supports Source B that there was a 'massacre', and gives broadly similar numbers ('over 300', where B says 347). Source B claims there were rapes, and C says: 'at least one rape'. Source C does not mention the killing of animals like Source B.*

However, Source A is less sure than Source C about the numbers killed (it says: 'at least 100'), and it does not mention rapes at all.

On balance, Source C mostly supports the evidence of Source B but there is much less agreement with Source A.

- Note the use of 'However'.
- Note the use of 'On balance' in the final sentence.

(c) How useful are Sources D and E as evidence about events at My Lai? (8)

TECHNIQUE

- You MUST mention the **provenance** and purpose of the sources to get a high mark.
- ALL sources are useful for something, even if they are not reliable.

Example: *Source D is useful because it proves that women and children were killed. It is especially useful because it was taken by the official American army photographer, who would have no reason to show such a photo (we might have doubted the photo if it had been taken by a **Vietcong** photographer). Source E is useful because it is an eye-witness account, although it is less trustworthy, because it is the memories of a villager and likely to be very biased.*

(d) 'The events at My Lai showed the US army to be bloodthirsty killers.' Use the sources and your own knowledge to explain whether you agree with this view. (12)

TECHNIQUE

- Don't just say whether you agree or disagree. First give the argument that suggests yes. Then give the argument that supports no.

- Don't go through the sources one after the other. Group them into those which support the point of view of the question and those which do not.

- You don't have to mention all the sources, but make sure you write about most of them.

- Use both the sources and your own knowledge, or you lose half the marks. You may want to flag up your own knowledge by starting the sentence with: 'From my own knowledge I know that . . .'

- Finish with a judgement. There isn't a right or wrong answer, but support your judgement by a short explanation.

Example conclusion: *In conclusion, there was a massacre at My Lai. Sources A–E all say so, and Source D proves it. From my own knowledge I know that William Calley was convicted for it. However, I also know that Hugh Thompson tried to stop the massacre, and Source F shows him getting a medal for this. So, it would not be true to say that all American soldiers were 'bloodthirsty killers'.*

- Note how the example does NOT use the words 'I think . . .'

AQA

The sources on which these examples are based are on pages 32–3.

(a) Why did President Johnson decide not stand for re-election in 1968? (6)

TECHNIQUE

- You need at least two good reasons (look at how many marks are available for this question).

- For each reason, try to give some facts, and you must explain how it led to Johnson's decision.

- Link your ideas together using words such as 'therefore', 'moreover', 'consequently', etc.

Example: *The first reason Johnson did not stand was because of the Tet Offensive. For a while, America had looked like it was losing, and America realised that the war would go on for a long time. They lost confidence in Johnson, and he therefore realised it was pointless standing for president – nobody would vote for him.*

Moreover, Johnson had had to cancel his Great Society programme to pay for the war. Civil Rights leaders such as Martin Luther King were unhappy about spending billions of dollars on the war when there was poverty at home in America. Johnson realised that he would not get their votes, so he decided not to stand.

Notice how one paragraph gives a military reason, and the second a political reason.

(b) Sources A and B give different views of the Vietnam War. Why do you think they are different? Explain your answer using Sources A and B and your own knowledge. (8)

TECHNIQUE

- Briefly say how the sources differ, but do not waste too much time comparing them – that is not the question.
- Make sure you use the provenance and purpose of the sources to help you explain your answer.
- Use some of your own knowledge to support your argument.
- Finish with a clear judgement as to why the sources are different, making sure you mention both sources.

Example conclusion: *In conclusion, it is common sense that President Johnson was going to defend his decision to abandon the Great Society programme. At the same time, it is obvious that Martin Luther King (who represented the poor people who needed the Great Society programme) was going to criticise it. This is why the two sources are so different.*

(c) How useful is Source C to an historian studying American attitudes towards the war? Use Source C and your own knowledge to answer this question. (8)

TECHNIQUE

- You need to make use of the source's provenance and purpose to score top marks. Think about the author's motives, i.e. why did he write this?
- You should also test how typical it was by comparing it with other sources and your own knowledge.
- You should also discuss the source's limitations – what else would you like to know?
- Don't confuse usefulness with reliability – a source can still be useful even if it isn't reliable.

Example: *This cartoon shows what one newspaper cartoonist of 1972 thought about Nixon. It shows him as fed up with a bad war. I know from my own knowledge that Nixon was desperate to get out of the war before the election, and that he used mass bombing as a way to force North Vietnam to make peace.*

However, this is just one newspaper, and we do not know whether this view of Nixon was shared by many people – to be sure, we would need to see other cartoons and comments by people from the time, and we would need to know how many people read the newspaper.

Note that, before you can answer a question about a cartoon, you need to decide what its meaning is.

(d) Why did opposition to the war increase? You may refer in your answer to:
- News of My Lai massacre
- Student protests
- Cost of the war. (8)

TECHNIQUE

- You need more than one reason, and you must back up each idea with facts and explanation.
- The bullet points are there to jog your memory. Make sure you mention them all, but also use your own ideas and knowledge.
- Finish with a judgement. There isn't a right or wrong answer, but support your judgement by a short explanation.

Example conclusion: *In conclusion, therefore, Americans opposed the war for many different reasons. Some thought it was immoral, others a waste of young American lives and money. Possibly, the most important reason was that it was a war America seemed to be losing.*

GLOSSARY

Artillery – cannons/big guns that fire shells at the enemy

ARVN – Army of the Republic of Vietnam (the South Vietnamese Army)

CIA – the American Central Intelligence Agency (government agents)

Civil Rights Movement – the movement which campaigns for equal rights and justice for American blacks

Commandos – soldiers trained to undertake dangerous stealth raids on or behind enemy lines

Communists – people who believe that the state should own the means of production

Concentration camps – prison camps

Credibility gap – the difference between what the government is telling people, and what they believe

Democracy – a system of government where people vote their leaders into power at an election

Desertion – running away from the army to avoid fighting

Draft – the American word for conscription (calling men up to join the army)

Draft-dodgers – those who avoid the draft by (for example) leaving the country or going into hiding

Free elections – elections that are not controlled by the government and where people really can vote for whomever they wish

Guerrilla – a type of soldier who uses hit-and-run tactics against the enemy and generally does not wear a uniform; these tactics are often used by weaker forces against a more powerful opponent in what is called a guerilla war

Guerrilla tactics – hit-and-run ambush tactics

Independence – where a country rules itself and is not controlled by a foreign power

Indo-China – the area of South East Asia comprising Vietnam, Laos and Cambodia

Infantry soldiers – foot soldiers

Ku Klux Klan – an extreme racist organisation from the American South

Napalm – an petroleum jelly used in bombs, which sticks to the skin and burns

Nationalists – people who love their country, and believe that it should be independent

National Liberation Front – (NLF) – North Vietnamese organisation which aimed to take over South Vietnam

Natural resources – raw materials, i.e. items (such as coal and rubber) needed by industry to make finished goods

North Vietnamese Army (NVA) – the regular army of North Vietnam

Outpost – a base deep in enemy territory

Parallel – the American word for a line of latitude on the map

Patriotic – love of one's country

Power vacuum – a situation where there is no obvious government/military force in power

Provenance – the provenance of a source is about who wrote it and when. Is there anything in the writer's background that makes his or her views more or less reliable? It is important for historians to know a source's provenance to help decide its reliability and value

Puppet state – a country, supposedly independent, but really controlled by a foreign power

Republic – a country which does not have a king or queen

Segregation – a policy whereby black people were not allowed to mix with white people

Supply lines – the ways in which an army is supplied with the food, weapons and other materials it needs

Vietminh – Vietnamese freedom fighters

Vietcong – American term for the Vietminh, designed to stress that they were communists

Vietnamisation – (also de-Americanisation) where the Americans began to pull out of the war, leaving the fighting more and more to the South Vietnamese

The publishers would like to thank the following individuals, institutions and companies for permission to reproduce copyright illustrations in this book:
Colorific p3; Robert Hunt Library p5; Bettman/Corbis p7; Corbis p8; Bettman/Corbis p9; Hulton Archive/Getty Images p11t; Bettman/Corbis p11b & p13; Associated Press p14; Bettman/Corbis p15; Don McCullin/Contact/nbpictures p17; Hulton Archive/Getty Images p19t; Corbis p19b; Philip Jones Griffiths/Magnum p21l; Don McCullin/Contact/nbpictures p21r; Marc Riboud/Magnum p23; Popperphoto p25; Corbis p26; Associated Press p27; Ronald L Haeberle p29l; Sipa Press/Rex Features p29r; Hulton Archive/Getty Images p31l; Bettman/Corbis p31r; Corbis p33l; St Paul Despatch/Fearing p33r; Hartford Times p35t; Sal Veder/Associated Press p35b; Bettman/Corbis p37 l&r; Vittoriano Rastelli/Corbis p39; Neil DeMarco p40 & 42.

All sources have been adapted to make them more accessible to students. The publishers would also like to thank the following for permission to reproduce material in this book:
Abacus, *The Bloody Game* by P Fussell; Appleton Century Crofts, *Documents of American History* by H S Commager; Ballantine Books, *Bloods* by W Terry & *Everything We Had* by A Santoli & *Lyndon: An Oral Biography* by M Miller; Bison Books, *Atlas of the Twentieth Century* by R Natkiel; Corgi, *Once A Warrior King: Memories of an Officer in Vietnam* by D Donovan; Harper Collins, *The Collins History of the World* by J A S Grenville & *Lyndon Johnson and the American Dream* by D Kearns; Hodder, *The USA and Vietnam* by V Sanders; I B Tauris, *Vietnam – A Portrait of its People at War* by D Chanoff & D Van Thoai; Longman, *America and the Vietnam War* by G J DeGroot; Orbis, *Guerrilla Warfare: From 1939 to the Present Day* by R Corbett; Osprey, *The Vietnam War 1956–75* by A Wiest; Oxford University Press, *A Concise History of the American Republic* by S E Morison, *et al*; Picador, *A Bright Shining Lie* by N Sheehan; Pimlico, *Vietnam – A History* by S Karnow; Presido, *A Life in a Year* by J R Ebert; *Salamander Books, The Vietnam War* by R L Bowers; *Time* magazine.

Every effort has been made to trace and acknowledge ownership of copyright. The publishers will be glad to make suitable arrangements with any copyright holders whom it has not been possible to contact.

Note about the Internet links in the book. The user should be aware that URLs or web addresses change regularly. Every effort has been made to ensure the accuracy of the URLs provided in this book on going to press. It is inevitable, however, that some will change. It is sometimes possible to find a relocated web page, by just typing in the address of the home page for a website in the URL window of your browser.

Orders: please contact Bookpoint Ltd, 130 Milton Park, Abingdon, Oxon OX14 4SB. Telephone: (44) 01235 827720. Fax: (44) 01235 400454. Lines are open from 9.00 – 6.00, Monday to Saturday, with a 24 hour message answering service. You can also order through our website www.hodderheadline.co.uk.

British Library Cataloguing in Publication Data
A catalogue record for this title is available from the British Library

ISBN 0 340 81476 4

First Published 2004
Impression number   10 9 8 7 6 5 4 3 2 1
Year   2010 2009 2008 2007 2006 2005 2004

Copyright © John D Clare 2004.

Cover photo from Tim Page/Corbis.
Typeset by Fakenham Photosetting Limited, Fakenham, Norfolk. Artwork on p2, 5, 6 and 25 by Art Construction.
Printed in Italy for Hodder & Stoughton Educational, a division of Hodder Headline, 338 Euston Road, London NW1 3BH.